Original title:
Healing the Soul of a Woman

Copyright © 2024 Swan Charm Publishing
All rights reserved.

Editor: Jessica Elisabeth Luik
Author: Liisi Lendorav
ISBN HARDBACK: 978-9916-86-048-9
ISBN PAPERBACK: 978-9916-86-049-6

Crimson Petals

Crimson petals in the breeze,
Gentle whispers through the trees,
Morning sun paints skies so bright,
Nature's canvas, pure delight.

Fragrance sweet, a perfume rare,
Dewdrops glisten, tender care,
Blossoms dance on velvet air,
Harmony beyond compare.

Soft enchantments, garden's grace,
Beauty in each sacred space,
Hearts that wander, find their place,
Crimson petals, love's embrace.

Woven Raindrops

Woven raindrops softly fall,
Nature's tears, a restful call,
Pattering on window panes,
Echoing in gentle strains.

Silver threads of liquid light,
Kissing earth in silent night,
Dreams awake, the world renew,
In the mist, a different view.

Every droplet spins a tale,
Through the storm, beyond the veil,
Life weaves magic, pure and true,
Woven raindrops, caught in blue.

Whirlwind Rest

Whirlwind rest upon the shore,
Silent waves forevermore,
Nature's breath in calm repose,
Secrets in the wind that knows.

Distant whispers speak of peace,
Turbulent hearts find release,
In the eye of storm's caress,
Solitude in stillness, bless.

Tranquil moments softly spin,
In the quiet, peace within,
Whirlwind's end, a sacred quest,
Finally, a place to rest.

Sunrise Silhouettes

Sunrise silhouettes on high,
Painting gold across the sky,
Morning's light, a tender hue,
Graceful dawn in shades of blue.

Shadows dance in first embrace,
Day awakens with such grace,
Horizon whispers, soft and clear,
Promises of warmth are near.

Dreams dissolve in morning's light,
Chasing darkness from the night,
Sunrise beckons, softly sets,
Anew the world, in silhouettes.

Guiding Fire

In the heart's deepest night,
A flame burns pure and bright.
Guiding spirits to their goal,
Igniting the dormant soul.

Whispers dance on the breeze,
Echoes of ancient seas.
Flames that never tire,
Beckon the inner fire.

In shadows cast by doubt,
A spark of light breaks out.
Ever constant this desire,
We follow the guiding fire.

Veins of Gold

Mountains tall and steep,
Secrets buried deep.
Within the earth so cold,
Lie veins of glittering gold.

Through time they silently wait,
Unchanged by fickle fate.
Strength in silence told,
Of hidden veins of gold.

To those who dare to seek,
Rivers of dreams will speak.
The brave shall behold,
Their glory in veins of gold.

Whispers of Renewal

In winter's icy grip,
Life takes a solemn dip.
Yet whispers through the trees,
Herald a warming breeze.

Beneath the frozen ground,
Seeds of hope are found.
Nature's quiet duel,
Brings whispers of renewal.

With spring's embrace so warm,
The world begins to transform.
In every bud and pool,
Echoes whispers of renewal.

Echoes of Inner Strength

In the silence of our mind,
Inner echoes we will find.
In struggles we are met,
Strength not seen, yet set.

Through the valleys we must tread,
Listening to voices unsaid.
Heart's whispers at great length,
Are echoes of inner strength.

When shadows cover light,
Hold to that silent might.
Resilient, we shall drink,
From echoes of inner strength.

Veiled Horizons

In twilight's veil, the sky unfolds,
Mystic dreams that time withholds.
Beyond the edge, where shadows play,
Horizons breathe, the end of day.

Stars ignite the cosmic seam,
Whispers soft like ancient steam.
Boundless, endless, night conceals,
Secrets that the twilight seals.

Moonlight dances, silver beams,
Kissing realms of hidden dreams.
Night's embrace, a silent cheer,
Veiled horizons, ever near.

Embrace of the Self

In the mirror of my soul,
Countless stories, endless whole.
Finding peace in silent breaths,
Inward journeys, life's true tests.

Soft reflections in my mind,
Echoes of the self defined.
In the stillness, I collide,
With the truths I can't abide.

Inner whispers guide my heart,
In this dance, I play my part.
Each embrace a chance to learn,
Inward steps, so gently turned.

Courageous Whispers

Whispers softly through the night,
Voices hidden out of sight.
Courage found in gentle sound,
In the shadows, strength is bound.

Secrets shared with quiet grace,
Fear and doubt they swift erase.
In the dark, the whispers bloom,
Courage breaks the silent gloom.

Every murmur, tender plea,
Forging paths for bravery.
Whispered words, a power grand,
Courage takes its fervent stand.

Strength in Silence

In the stillness of the dawn,
Strength in silence, softly drawn.
Echoes held within the breast,
Silent nights where fears can rest.

Calm and poised, the silence speaks,
Fills the heart when courage peaks.
In the quiet, strength is found,
Every breath, a sacred ground.

Solitude, a friend in need,
Places where the soul is freed.
In the silence, power grows,
Strength in calm, the spirit knows.

Whispers of Resilience

In the stillness of the night,
A whisper softly speaks,
Of battles fought in silence,
Of strengths yet to peak.

Through storms and blazing fires,
Through thorns and rugged trails,
A heart that's forged by trials,
In each beat, it never fails.

Among the fallen shadows,
Where once despair had grown,
A light begins to shimmer,
From seeds of hope now sown.

In valleys deep and mournful,
Where echoes faintly ring,
The whisper grows in might,
As resilience starts to sing.

From ashes of the broken,
From tears that carve the face,
Rise whispers of resilience,
In eternal strong embrace.

Renewed Wings

By the dawn's first gentle light,
A new horizon gleams,
The night has softly whispered,
Of newly crafted dreams.

Through winds that test and try,
With wings spread wide and high,
From shadows past emerge,
To grasp the open sky.

The heart now finds its rhythm,
With every beat it sings,
Of past, and present melding,
To form renewed wings.

In the cascade of moments,
Where past and future meet,
New wings unfold and flutter,
As courage finds its feet.

No longer bound by sorrow,
No longer held by strings,
Soar high, embrace tomorrow,
With ever-renewed wings.

Echoes of Inner Strength

In the quiet of the morning,
Before the world awakes,
Echoes of an inner strength,
Resound as spirit shakes.

Past the walls of hardship's hold,
Through battles fought within,
No longer bound by silent chains,
The strength begins to win.

From deep within the chambers,
Where courage oft is found,
A voice of hope emerges,
In harmony profound.

Each step now grows in power,
With every breath, a spark,
Of inner strength's resilience,
That brightens life's arc.

In moments of reflection,
Where shadows softly blend,
Echoes of inner strength,
Declare a will to mend.

Blossoms of Serenity

Within the garden's quiet,
Where peace and silence dwell,
Blossoms of serenity,
Have stories yet to tell.

The petals whisper gently,
In breezes soft and mild,
Of days when storms have quieted,
And hearts are reconciled.

In every shade and color,
A symphony of calm,
A soothing balm for weary souls,
In nature's open palm.

Amid the tranquil stillness,
Where time seems to take flight,
Blossoms of serenity,
Bloom softly in the light.

Here every moment lingers,
In sweet serenity's glow,
Where peace and grace converge,
And inner quiet grows.

Blossoms in the Night

Under moon's gentle light,
Petals whisper dreams so bright.
Stars reflect in dew-kissed glow,
Nature's secret nighttime show.

Shadows dance in whispered song,
Silent whispers all night long.
Blossoms open, soft and true,
In the night, their colors grew.

Midnight air, so crisp and clear,
Whispers stories we hold dear.
Nighttime blooms, their fragrance spreads,
Dreams arise from flower beds.

Among the stars, flowers bloom,
Nature's art in twilight's room.
Blossoms glow, the world asleep,
Nighttime's secrets, dreams we keep.

Silence Between Heartbeats

In the quiet, in between,
Moments where the truth is seen.
Heartbeats whisper soft and low,
In the silence, feelings grow.

Paused in time, a tender space,
Heartbeat's echo, love's embrace.
In that stillness, clear and bright,
Love's true form comes into sight.

Breathing in the quiet calm,
Heart and soul in gentle balm.
Between the beats, life slows down,
Silent whispers all around.

In the gaps where silence lies,
Whispers turn to silent cries.
Heartbeats steady, love anew,
Silence speaks the deepest truth.

Wings of Resilience

Through the storm, we rise and soar,
Strength within, forevermore.
Wings of hope and dreams untold,
In our hearts, brave stories hold.

Challenges like tempests rage,
Yet we turn another page.
Wings of resilience lift us high,
Toward the ever-changing sky.

In adversity, we find,
Strength of heart and peace of mind.
Wings spread wide, with courage true,
Facing skies of brilliant blue.

With each trial, our spirits climb,
Soaring through the sands of time.
Wings of resilience, bold and bright,
Guide us through the darkest night.

Rivers of Transformation

Flowing waters, ever-changing,
In their depths, life rearranging.
Rivers carve both rock and clay,
Shaping paths both night and day.

In their currents, stories blend,
Beginnings, journeys without end.
Rivers deep in constant flow,
In their heart, the secrets know.

From the mountains to the sea,
Rivers speak of what will be.
Transformation in their course,
Tracing nature's living force.

Rivers run with purpose, true,
Changing old to something new.
In their waters, life renews,
Rivers flow with endless views.

Seeds of Courage

In the heart of shadowed glen,
Bloom seeds of courage, then and when.
Fear not the path ahead so fraught,
For strength within is not for naught.

Roots dig deep in soil so tough,
Through harshest winds they won't rebuff.
From tiny seeds, great trees arise,
Reaching ever towards the skies.

Faces turned to dawn's first light,
Boldly standing through the blight.
Whispering leaves in quiet might,
Each heartbeats strong, each resolve tight.

When tempests roar and skies grow dark,
Remember seeds that made their mark.
For courage blossoms in the night,
Guiding us to morning's light.

Waves of Serenity

Upon the boundless sea they play,
Waves, serene, call night and day.
Softly lapping at the shore,
A symphony forevermore.

In tranquil tones, they gently speak,
To restless souls both brave and meek.
Horizons vast, a dreamscape blue,
Whispering the old and new.

Silent drift on ocean wide,
A dance beneath the lunar tide.
Serenity in every crest,
A lullaby that offers rest.

Amber dusk and dawning hue,
Paint with calm each moment true.
In every wave, a story told,
Of peace within the waters hold.

Cradle of Stars

In the velvet cradle of the night,
Stars are woven, pure and bright.
Each gleam, a story carved in time,
Distant echoes, soft and sublime.

The cosmos sings in silent praise,
Guiding dreams through skies' vast maze.
Infinite whispers, ancient lore,
Galaxies dance, forevermore.

Constellations, threads of light,
Weave the tapestry of night.
Guiding wanderers lost in thought,
To realms beyond, where dreams are sought.

In the cradle of stars, hearts find peace,
A vast expanse where worries cease.
Gazing up, we touch the skies,
Finding hope in twinkling eyes.

True North Awakens

Upon the compass, true north calls,
Guiding through life's rise and falls.
In the silence, hearts awaken,
By unseen paths we are taken.

Through wild terrains and forests deep,
Where whispered secrets softly seep.
True north awakens, inner sight,
To bravely wander into night.

With stars as guides and winds a song,
Leading travelers all along.
To find the purpose, pure and keen,
In every leaf and every scene.

Awakening from slumber's dream,
We follow north, a timeless theme.
For in the quest we find our way,
True north awakens day by day.

Threads of Hope

In the fabric of night, stars are spun
Each thread a whisper, a wish begun
Through darkest eves, a silver seam
Weaves dreams together, a radiant beam

Hands of fate sew what we yearn
In tattered hearts, embers burn
From every tear, a tapestry grows
In hope's embrace, sorrow glows

Over the horizon, dawn's tender kiss
Casts shadows back, ignites bliss
Glimmers of possibility, brightly scoped
In life's loom, threads of hope

In silence, strength we find
Mysteries of destiny, intertwined
With courage's needle, fears elope
Crafting tomorrows from threads of hope

Wounds to Wisdom

In scars, stories softly told
Of battles fought, of hearts bold
Etched in flesh, lessons lie
From pain's ashes, spirits rise

Wounds whisper truths profound
In silence, wisdom is found
Each cut a chapter, each bruise a verse
Pain fades, but insights immerse

Through turmoil's haze, we seek the light
Find strength in shadows, in darkened flight
Sorrow's chisel, wisdom's mold
From wounds, the wise unfold

With time, raw edges smooth
In healing's cradle, souls soothe
From every fall, we rise again
Turn wounds to wisdom, forgone pain

Infinite Blossoms

In gardens of endless bloom
Under sun and moon's soft plume
Petals weave a tapestry bright
Infinite blossoms, day and night

Each flower a dream set free
In the winds, a symphony
Life's essence in colors bestowed
In endless meadows, love is sowed

Spring's gentle breath revives
Nature's touch, all that thrives
A canvas of hope unfurls
In infinite blossoms, worlds twirl

Through seasons, they remain
A cycle of joy after rain
In every bloom, stories we see
Infinite blossoms, eternity

Mending the Mirror

Shattered glass reflects the soul's plight
In broken shards, stories ignite
With tender hands, pieces we bind
Mending the mirror, hearts aligned

Fragments of past, moments arrayed
Through each crack, light is conveyed
In imperfections, beauty gleams
Mending the mirror, mending dreams

Every piece holds a tale untold
Of love and pain, of hearts bold
In the mosaic, truths we find
Mending the mirror, peace of mind

With every touch, scars are healed
True reflections are revealed
Unity in fragments, we adhere
Mending the mirror, we see clear

Luminous Dawn

The sky is bathed in golden hues,
As morning rays play peek-a-boo,
Nighttime shadows softly fuse,
With daybreak's promise, fresh and new.

Whispers of the world awake,
Birdsong fills the tranquil air,
Each moment, a gentle ache,
Of beauty or of silent prayer.

Petals open to the light,
Their vibrant colors softly gleam,
Everything feels pure and right,
In the glow of dawn's first beam.

Mountains kissed by amber blush,
Valleys wrapped in tender mist,
In this serene morning hush,
Nature's splendor can't be missed.

It's a time for hope to grow,
For dreams to take their flight,
In the golden dawn's warm glow,
Lies a world both soft and bright.

Velvet Shadows

In the shade where secrets whisper low,
Shadows dance a silent tune,
Beneath the moon's soft-glowing glow,
Night's mysteries gently croon.

Stars are pearls on blackened silk,
Sleeping world in calm embrace,
Dreams are spun like threads of milk,
Flowing in this tender space.

Whispers weave through midnight air,
Velvet shadows come alive,
Soft as kisses, none compare,
To the night where phantoms thrive.

Every corner holds a tale,
Hidden in the dusky light,
Mystery in shadows pale,
Enigmas of the darkened night.

Soft and silent are the dreams,
That within the dark abide,
In those velvet shadowed seams,
Truth and fantasy reside.

Sacred Pathways

Under arching, ancient trees,
Paths of wisdom stretch ahead,
Through whispered winds and gentle breeze,
Secrets of the earth are spread.

Stone by stone, the journey calls,
With each step, a sacred thread,
Echoes of the ages fall,
From the path that we must tread.

Mystic symbols carved in bark,
Guiding us through past and now,
In the daylight and the dark,
Sacred pathways show us how.

Tread softly on this hallowed ground,
With reverence in every stride,
For in each place, a truth is found,
Hidden just where shadows slide.

In this journey, hearts entwined,
With the earth and sky and more,
Seek and you shall truly find,
What these pathways have in store.

Tender Valleys

Softly spread 'neath mountain's hold,
Valleys whisper tender lore,
Streams of silver, veins of gold,
In their bosom, treasures store.

Fields of green and flowers bright,
Painted by a delicate hand,
In their soft and tranquil light,
Beauty breathes across the land.

Echoes sound of past-day songs,
Winds of olden tales unfold,
In the valley where heart belongs,
Stories timeless, softly told.

Petals kiss the morning dew,
As day awakes in gentle yawn,
Tender valleys' charm anew,
In the early blush of dawn.

Cradled in this peaceful womb,
Life finds solace, heart finds grace,
In the valley's quiet bloom,
Love and nature interlace.

Garlands of Renewal

In gardens where the dawn awakes,
whispered secrets in the dew,
life finds paths through tangled fates,
reclaiming cycles bold and new.

Winds bring songs of fresh reprise,
leaves in chorus, green and bright,
radiance beneath the skies,
adorn the earth with morning's light.

Roots embrace the fertile ground,
ancient soils, stories told,
through the seasons, round and round,
birth and death in patterns bold.

Petals bloom in fragrant dance,
echoes of the times once past,
each revival, a second chance,
with love and hope, hearts hold fast.

In the twilight, shadows fall,
colors fade, yet spirits rise,
through it all, we heed the call,
rekindle flames that never die.

Shimmering Through Shadows

Threads of light in twilight's weave,
shadowed pathways, steps unseen,
journeys taken, where we grieve,
find the places we have been.

Stars above in silent stoic,
glide through nights, so cold and vast,
in their gaze, we're catatonic,
moments fleeting, never last.

Echoes whisper through the night,
soft assurances, whispers bold,
from the dark, emerge the light,
hidden truths begin to unfold.

Moonlight casts its silver veil,
covers dreams in soft repose,
through the shadows, voices wail,
tales of sorrow, joy, and woes.

In the black, reflections gleam,
dancing forms in silhouette,
through the dark, we start to dream,
promise of dawn yet unmet.

Harmony of Becoming

From the silence, notes arise,
melodies of self embrace,
unseen chords beneath the skies,
in the heart, a sacred space.

Tides of change, relentless flow,
sculpting arcs of destiny,
in the rhythm, we all grow,
find our place in unity.

Voices blend, a chorus grand,
harmonies in sync with time,
through the song, we understand,
love and grace in perfect rhyme.

Paths converge and then diverge,
scripts of life in symphony,
as we listen, we emerge,
part of this vast tapestry.

In each note, a story told,
echoes of our journey's truth,
in the harmony, we hold,
wisdom's whisper, spirit's youth.

Prisms of Self-Worth

Crystals catch the morning light,
fractals spread in endless dance,
refracting truths within our sight,
deep within, a second glance.

In the mirror, see the glow,
facets gleaming, sharp and bright,
know your value, let it show,
every angle, perfect light.

Rainbows arc with vibrant hues,
colors merge in unity,
in their beauty, find your muse,
paint your worth in harmony.

Strength residing, inner core,
never dim beneath life's weight,
diamond heart, through pain, it's more,
resilient, strong, it's innate.

Face the world with lifted chin,
self-reflection crystal clear,
know your worth lies deep within,
shine your light, dispel the fear.

Forgotten Lullabies

In dreams of yesteryears, they hum
Soft whispers of a mother's song
Through twilight's veil, in shadows come
Where memories eternally belong

Beneath the starlit, velvet sky
They weave the tales of night's embrace
And as the silver moon drifts by
They bid the sorrows to efface

The echoes of a distant tune
In melodies of old reside
By night's caress and day's cocoon
In slumber's arms, the past we bide

When silence deepens, close your eyes
Embrace the voice that time denies
For there within the night's disguise
Live whispers of forgotten lullabies

Heartstrings Rewoven

A tapestry of love we weave
With threads of joy and strands of pain
Across the times, the heart believes
In every sun, in every rain

Through tangled knots and frayed design
Resilient is the hope we keep
Each stitch of laughter, tear to bind
In woven dreams we rise, we leap

When shadows darken, days grow cold
The heartstrings pull with fervent might
In intricate patterns, tales retold
Of love's enduring, hidden light

With every beat, the fabric mends
In silent whispers, secrets spun
For love's embrace, a truth transcends
A story reawakened, never done

Veils of Clarity

Beneath the mists of morning's gaze
A world unseen emerges bright
In valued truths through softened haze
The shadows fall to dawn's first light

Through veils of doubt and whispered fear
Piercing clarity prevails
And with each step, we draw them near
The path unveiled, our spirit sails

In moments where the fog retreats
We find the wisdom deep inside
For knowledge grows when mind entreats
And clouds of doubt no longer hide

Beyond the shrouds, the vision clear
The heart aligned with mind's decree
In timeless space where truth appears
Lie veils of clarity, set free

Waves in Still Water

In tranquil seas, where silence lays
The ripples whisper tales of old
With gentle embrace, the water sways
Through timeless depths, the secrets told

Each breath in harmony aligns
With whispers of the waves serene
In peace profound, the soul refines
A dance unseen, a force unseen

The quiet speaks with tender grace
In moments where the mind's at rest
The waves may stir in their own pace
In stillness known, the heart is blessed

For in the mirror of the deep
Reflections of the world we trace
And as the waters softly sweep
We find our peace, our sacred space

Moonlit Reflections

The moon whispers secrets, so calm and so bright,
Guiding the weary through velvet night.
Stars dance in silence, a celestial arc,
Painting dreams on the canvas dark.

Beneath the moon's glow, shadows softly play,
Revealing truths hidden by the day.
Quiet waves lap at the shore,
Singing tales of forevermore.

Silver beams kiss the forest deep,
Where ancient trees their wisdom keep.
Owl's call pierces the tranquil air,
A guardian of the twilight's prayer.

In this stillness, hearts find their rest,
Cradled by night in nature's breast.
Moonlit reflections gentle minds,
A serene escape from life's confines.

As dawn approaches, night bids adieu,
With a promise to return anew.
In the dance of sun and moon,
Our souls find balance tuned.

Sunrise Within

Golden light on the horizon breaks,
Awakening dreams in quiet lakes.
Shadows retreat as skies ignite,
A whispered promise of dawn's first light.

Mountains stand tall, kissed by the sun,
A day's new journey has just begun.
Birds sing praises to morning's grace,
Filling the air with life's embrace.

Warmth spreads through the waking land,
A gentle touch from time's own hand.
Flowers bloom with petals wide,
Opening hearts to the day inside.

In the hush of morning's birth,
We find the glow of our own worth.
A spark within, tender and true,
Guiding us through skies of blue.

As the sun climbs higher still,
We harness the strength of will.
With each sunrise comes a chance,
To live, to love, to life enhance.

Symphony of Scars

In the quiet echoes of life's refrain,
Where joy and sorrow both remain.
A tapestry of wounds we bear,
Each scar a note, a song laid bare.

Trials carved with pain and strife,
Compose the symphony of life.
Resilient hearts, despite the scars,
Shine with the brilliance of distant stars.

Music born from whispered pleas,
A melody upon the breeze.
Lessons learned in silent night,
Give voice to souls that seek the light.

Every wound that we embrace,
Forms a harmony, finds its place.
Together we create a tune,
A resonant, healing afternoon.

In the concert of our days,
We find healing in subtle ways.
A symphony of scars we sing,
A testament to what life can bring.

Rains of Forgiveness

Soft rain falls, a cleansing touch,
Washing away the burdened clutch.
Each droplet whispers tales untold,
Of hearts that learn to be bold.

Quiet patter on the earth's face,
A hymn of mercy, gentle grace.
Past mistakes in rivulets flow,
Toward a future where kindness grows.

Through the storm, we find release,
In the rain, our souls find peace.
Baptized in forgiveness' gentle sway,
We learn to let the shadows fade.

Clouds part to reveal the sun,
A new dawn where healing's begun.
Tears once shed in sorrow's grasp,
Now nourish roots that firmly clasp.

In the symphony of falling rain,
We find solace from the pain.
Rains of forgiveness cleanse the past,
Creating spaces where love can last.

Echoes of Rebirth

In stillness where the shadows sleep,
A whisper calls from depths untold,
The echoes of a past we keep,
In mem'ries wrapped, in dreams we hold.

From ashes gray, new life unfolds,
The dawn arise on golden breath,
And in each heart, a truth embold,
A dance between the life and death.

A river winds through ancient stone,
With ripples soft, the past it weaves,
The currents carve in whispered tone,
A tapestry of eyes that grieve.

Yet in the silent beats, reborn,
With gentle grace, the night recedes,
The dawn anew, the morn adorn,
With rays of hope, with nature's seeds.

Embrace of the Phoenix

Through the flames, the heart ignites,
A spirit forged from burning skies,
With wings ablaze, it takes to heights,
In fiery dance of endless rise.

The ashes fall, the past becalms,
In embers' glow, a life renews,
A symphony of silent psalms,
In every breath, a hope imbues.

The darkness yields to dawn's embrace,
With feathers pure, it soars above,
A journey born from trial's grace,
A testament of endless love.

In cyclical rebirth, it finds,
A lesson writ in ancient lore,
Through time and space, the spirit binds,
And lives are changed forevermore.

Garden of Desires

In twilight's hush, where shadows play,
A garden blooms with whispered dreams,
Each petal soft in moon's display,
Reflects a world not what it seems.

Within the maze, desires thread,
Through vine and bloom, a heart's delight,
Each fragrant wish in twilight spread,
A silent dance beneath the night.

The flowers bloom with secret song,
Their colors weave in passion's hue,
In every scent, desires long,
A tapestry of love anew.

Beneath the stars, the garden sighs,
Its beauty speaks in gentle breeze,
And in its depths, the heart complies,
To nature's call, to fond reprise.

Threads of Hope

On loom of dreams, the threads entwine,
With colors bold and spirits bright,
In every stitch, a life divine,
A tapestry of endless light.

Through heartache's veils, the yarn persists,
To weave a cloth of love and grace,
In every strand, a hope insists,
To heal the wounds time can't erase.

The weaver's hand, both firm and kind,
Guides every thread with gentle care,
In fabric's touch, a peace we find,
In each embrace, a hope laid bare.

And through the years, the cloth expands,
With every soul, a thread aligns,
Connecting hearts across the lands,
In patterns pure, where love defines.

Boundaries of Serenity

In the hush of twilight's grace,
Whispers drift on zephyrs mild,
Hearts find solace, minds embrace,
Peace like innocence of a child.

Beyond the murmurs of the day,
Where worries fade, a tender grin,
A sanctuary far away,
Deep within, true calm begins.

In the touch of evening's hue,
Painted skies, a tranquil art,
Harmony in shades of blue,
Easing the most restless heart.

Souls unfurl like morning blooms,
Fragile dreams on twilight's brink,
In these still and quiet rooms,
Tides of thought, in peace, we sink.

Boundaries that gently close,
Hold us like a warm embrace,
Serenity in soft repose,
Finds us in this sacred space.

Melodies of Belief

Notes like stars in evening's glow,
Cascade gentle from the heights,
Faith and hope in rhythms flow,
Guiding through the darkest nights.

Echoes of forgotten songs,
Stir the heart and soothe the mind,
In that flow, where time belongs,
Sacred themes of trust we find.

Strings of fate in harmony,
Weaving tales of ancient lore,
Melodies of certainty,
Resonate forevermore.

Harmony in whispers sweet,
Softly heals the weary soul,
In each chord our dreams do meet,
Making fractured spirits whole.

Belief like a steadfast stream,
Through life's valleys, ever true,
Melodies that form a dream,
Carry us beyond the blue.

Dreamscapes of the Heart

In the quiet of the night,
When the world is still and calm,
Dreams take wings in silver light,
Bearing visions, pure as psalm.

Wandering through fields of gold,
Hearts embark on journeys vast,
Stories of the soul unfold,
Moments captured, meant to last.

Stars above in tender gaze,
Guide the dreamer's wayward flight,
Mystic paths where moonlight plays,
Weaving wonders in the night.

Silent whispers, sweet and low,
Echo through the dreamer's mind,
Hopes like rivers gently flow,
In this realm, purest we find.

Dreamscapes of the heart entwine,
Threads of fate and whispered cheer,
In the night, our spirits shine,
Finding solace, true and clear.

Candlelight Rekindled

In the flicker, shadows play,
Dancing flames, a soft embrace,
Warmth and light of yesterday,
Fill the room with gentle grace.

Memories in amber glow,
Whispers of a time once dear,
In each flicker, moments show,
Love that lingers ever near.

Eyes reflect the candle's gleam,
Hearts aglow with tender light,
In this sacred, quiet dream,
Darkness bows to gentle might.

Softly, hope is rekindled,
In the glow of candle's hue,
Where once doubts and fears swindled,
Now the heart begins anew.

Candlelight, a guiding star,
Through the night, a beacon bright,
Reminds us, no matter how far,
Love returns with morning's light.

Rivers of Renewal

Upon the banks where dreams unfold,
In waters clear and stories old,
Rivers carve their timeless song,
Carrying hopes and fears along.

A leaf's brief dance on currents swift,
As seasons change, their gifts they lift,
Renewed by time and nature's hand,
They sculpt anew the shifting sand.

From mountain peaks to ocean's call,
Through valleys deep, where shadows fall,
Their whispers speak of life renewed,
In every drop, a world imbued.

Eternal flows that cleanse and guide,
Beneath the sky, so open wide,
In mirrored depths, reflection's grace,
A liquid path through time and space.

Wherever flows this liquid thread,
In silver streams on earth's wide bed,
We find in rivers' endless flow,
A cycle vast, where life seeds grow.

Celestial Harmony

Beneath the dome of twinkling light,
Stars weave their tales in velvet night,
A cosmic dance of fire and grace,
Unveiling secrets in deep space.

Constellations whisper lore,
Of ancient times and love once bore,
In silent symphony above,
A testament to boundless love.

Planets twirl in rhythmic beat,
Their orbits sing a tune so sweet,
Eclipsing shadows, moonlit hue,
A ballet in the midnight blue.

Galaxies in spiraled form,
In aeons past and futures born,
Craft a canvas vast and grand,
Wonders drawn by divine hand.

In this expanse, so wide and free,
We gaze upon infinity,
And in the starlight's gentle glow,
Our place within the stars we know.

Inner Landscapes

Within the mind, vast plains extend,
Where thoughts and dreams and memories blend,
A tapestry of hopes and fears,
Woven through the passing years.

Mountains rise in moments bold,
Peaks of triumph, valleys cold,
Emotions like a river flow,
Through landscapes only we can know.

Forests dense with secrets kept,
Paths where shadows softly crept,
In every leaf a whispered tale,
In every breeze, a heart's exhale.

The desert's quiet, endless space,
Echoes of a tranquil grace,
Where silence speaks in sandy sighs,
Beneath the wide and open skies.

Within these realms, the soul finds peace,
In inner worlds, where worries cease,
A journey through the mind's terrain,
In search of self, we come again.

Whispers of Granite

In silent strength, the mountains stand,
With whispers carved by nature's hand,
Granite peaks that touch the sky,
Guardians of the world on high.

Through ages past, their forms were cast,
In timeless stone, a story vast,
Of earth's great power, calm and wild,
Each crag and cliff a history filed.

Canyons deep with shadows long,
Echoes faint of ancient song,
Where winds have sculpted, rain has kissed,
Textures rough, by time persist.

Ice and sun in cycles play,
On granite faces worn and grey,
Yet in their stoic, silent grace,
There's wisdom in each weathered face.

Mountains tall and valleys deep,
In their embrace, old secrets sleep,
And in their quiet, steadfast might,
We find both awe and deep delight.

Fires of Transformation

In embers' glow, we find our source,
Through flames, life's changing force.
Ash becomes a fertile ground,
From scorched earth, new hope is found.

Phoenix rises from the blaze,
In fiery dance, we find new ways.
Burn away the old and frail,
Through the fire, we prevail.

Depths of Understanding

Beneath the waves, where silence speaks,
Answers hide, in shadows deep.
Eyes closed, feel the soul's embrace,
In the depths, we find our place.

Mysteries weave in ocean's curl,
Thoughts like pearls, in a whorl.
Submerge the mind, let go of fear,
True wisdom whispers here.

Petals of Grace

Petals drift on autumn's breeze,
Capture moments, such simple ease.
Soft and tender, they unfold,
Stories of life's grace retold.

Whispers of what lies ahead,
Blooming paths that we tread.
Fragile beauty marks our trace,
In each petal, we find grace.

Wind's Gentle Murmur

The wind whispers secrets low,
Through the trees, it gently flows.
Carrying thoughts on silent wings,
Nature's voice in softest strings.

Leaves dance in a waltz unseen,
Songs of old in every green.
Breathe in deep, the murmurs tell,
Life's quiet symphony, all is well.

Rainbows of Self-Discovery

In the quiet dawn's embrace,
I find colors in my heart's place.
Whispers of dreams, so vivid, so true,
A spectrum of me, each hue, each clue.

Soft glows of hope, bright beams of grace,
Paint a path through time, leaving no trace.
With every new arc, my soul does wake,
To realms unknown, each step I take.

Mysteries unfold in the skies above,
Echoes of laughter, shadows of love.
In the mirrored pool, my reflection blooms,
A journey unfolds beyond the glooms.

Seeking solace in the rain's caress,
A dance of light in moments of distress.
Unveiling secrets buried deep within,
Where a rainbow starts, where dreams begin.

Colors blend in a symphony untold,
Stories of courage, hearts bold.
In the rainbow's arc, I find my way,
To self-discovery with each new day.

Embers of Wisdom

Silent whispers of a fiery core,
Old tales of yore, legends and lore.
In the embers' glow, wisdom speaks,
Silent voices, time's mystique.

From the ashes of yesterday's fight,
Rise insights veiled in the night.
With each flicker, truths emerge,
Guiding through the dark, an endless urge.

Ancient eyes cradled in the glow,
See beyond what minds can know.
Lessons buried in the glowing ember,
Ignite the soul, make it remember.

In the stillness of the dying flame,
Lies resilience, never tame.
Whispers of time in the ember's hue,
Whispering wisdom, ancient and true.

From the sparks of a kindred fire,
Rise desires that never tire.
Embers of wisdom, burning bright,
Guide the spirit through the night.

Gates of Inner Peace

Through gates adorned with tranquil scenes,
Lie the answers to all one's means.
A gentle breeze, a calming sigh,
In the stillness, spirits fly.

Paths of silence, meadows so wide,
Inward journeys, a quiet guide.
With every step, a burden sheds,
Through whispers of peace, the heart treads.

Stillness wraps in an embrace,
Slows the breath, softens the pace.
Among the quiet, the mind finds cease,
Unveiled truths, purest peace.

In every leaf, a lesson lies,
In every breeze, a soul's sigh.
Through these gates, the seeking cease,
In the heart's calm, we find peace.

Hushed echoes of an inner grace,
Fill the void, its gentle space.
Gates of calm, the fears release,
Through them, we find inner peace.

Shadows of Redemption

In shadows deep, where light is rare,
Lies a story none would dare.
Of second chances, hopes redeemed,
In twilight's touch, the spirit's dream.

In the dark, the echoes call,
From a past where shadows fall.
But in the depths, redemption's near,
Through shadow's dance, paths made clear.

A journey back from broken ground,
To where light and hope are found.
In every fall, a rise anew,
In shadow's grasp, the spirit grew.

Forgiveness whispers through the shade,
Of past mistakes, of debts unpaid.
In every trial, redemption parses,
Uniting souls, mending tarses.

From darkness springs a hope so bright,
Guiding lost souls to the light.
In shadows' depths, redemption's blend,
A story twisted, with a happy end.

Hallowed Grounds

In whispers of the morning dew,
Ancient tales are softly strewn,
On paths where scholars once did trod,
And dreams commune with hallowed gods.

Elders' breath in amber light,
Guides the lost through troubled night,
In chiseled stone and verdant glades,
Eternal wisdom never fades.

Beneath the canopy of stars,
Echoes linger from afar,
Where shadows dance and secrets lie,
And ancient spirits softly cry.

Time enshrines both good and ill,
In sacred ground, the earth stands still,
Guardians of the olden lore,
In silent reverence evermore.

Step with care on hallowed grounds,
Where history with faith abounds,
Bound by time in whispered prayer,
Eternal solace, granted there.

Transforming Tides

By the shore with whispering waves,
Time in cycles, nature paves,
Changing hues and shifting sands,
Shape the edges, form new lands.

Moonlit nights and sunlit days,
In cosmic dance the water sways,
Bringing forth the briny air,
And secrets ancient, laid repair.

Currents weave their silent might,
In twilight's grace and dawn's first light,
Stories washed from distant shores,
Held in depths forevermore.

Oceans sing their timeless song,
Of life's embrace, the right and wrong,
In the ebb and flow, we see,
A mirror of humanity.

In each swell and each retreat,
Find the strength to rise, defeat,
For within transforming tides,
A boundless spirit still abides.

Amber Glow

In the heart of twilight's grace,
Amber hues the night embrace,
Candlelight in whispers glows,
Where the truth of evening shows.

Leaves bathed in a golden gleam,
Embrace the earth in quiet dream,
Sunset's fire, soft and warm,
Holds our spirits, safe from harm.

Reflections dance on waters still,
Gentle light our fears distill,
In this hour of calm repose,
Find the peace the soul bestows.

Fading day to tranquil night,
Leaves behind a tender light,
In the amber glow, we find,
The tender touch of time, so kind.

Moments held in twilight's cast,
Speak of loves that truly last,
In the golden hour's flow,
Heart to heart, the fires grow.

Gentle Storms

Beneath the clouds, a thrum of rain,
In patterns soft, a sweet refrain,
Whispers in the quiet night,
Nature's touch, serene and light.

Thunder rolls with tender care,
In the winds, a silent prayer,
Raindrops on the leaves' embrace,
Kiss the earth with gentle grace.

Lightning's flash in muted tones,
Illuminates the skies' vast zones,
Guides the heart through tempest's veil,
Where softest whispers tell their tale.

Storms that pass with tender might,
Cleanse the soul, renew its light,
In the calm that follows soon,
Find the peace of dusk and moon.

Embrace the storm, both fierce and kind,
In its arms, a rest you'll find,
In the gentle storm's embrace,
Feel the touch of life's sweet grace.

Rivers of Reflection

In twilight's gentle, quiet stream,
Whispers of past and future gleam,
Flowing with secrets, dreams unfold,
Stories in waters, softly told.

Cradled by banks of time and stone,
Where solitude is gently sown,
Mirrors of sky in liquid prose,
Revealing truths the mind bestows.

Ripples weave patterns of the heart,
Tracing the arcs where lives depart,
Murmurs of hope, echoes of pain,
Dancing in time with soft refrain.

Journey through calm and tempest wild,
Cradling fragments of life compiled,
In every surge, a lesson learned,
In every turn, a soul returned.

From source to sea, the rivulets blend,
Marking beginnings that meet their end,
A winding path, a glistening beam,
Rivers of thought in liquid dream.

Wings of Renewal

From silent slumber, rise anew,
From shadowed past, the light breaks through,
On wings of change, our spirits soar,
Embracing what was lost before.

Transforming whispers on the breeze,
A symphony among the trees,
Each feathered flight a new refrain,
Of lives reborn from shades of pain.

In pastel dawns and setting suns,
The cycle of renewal runs,
Each step, a path to something more,
Each flight, a door to yesteryore.

Beyond the clouds, horizons clear,
With every beat, we cast off fear,
In the embrace of azure sky,
On wings of hope, we learn to fly.

Soar ever higher, dreams unfurled,
Renewed, reborn into the world,
With wings that touch the edges bright,
We chase the fading edge of night.

Destined Petals

Upon the garden's tender face,
Unfolding petals find their place,
Each bloom a tale of time's decree,
A whispered prologue, silently.

In hues of dawn and twilight's blush,
A story weaves in fragrant hush,
From sheltered bud to full display,
Destiny in each bright array.

Soft petals trace the arc of fate,
From summer's grin to autumn's gate,
Embracing moments, seasons fleet,
Life's transient pulse, both soft and sweet.

Through storms that bend and winds that cleave,
In steadfast grace, they do not grieve,
For in each fall, a promise cast,
That life renews beyond the past.

In gardens vast and meadows wide,
Destined petals bloom with pride,
A cycle spun on nature's thread,
In every blossom, futures spread.

Veins of Resilience

In every leaf and every stem,
A silent strength lies deep within,
Veins of resilience subtly trace,
The pathways of an unsung grace.

Through drought and storm, through blight and glee,
A tale of fortitude we see,
In veins that pulse with life's pure thread,
A will to thrive where others dread.

Against the winds that harshly blow,
Through trials only the strong will know,
Nature's resolve does not relent,
In every strain, in every bent.

Emerging from the cracks of stone,
In places desolate, alone,
Resilience finds a way to show,
In stubborn shoots that sprout and grow.

So let us learn from nature's way,
That even in the darkest day,
Through veins of strength, our spirits mend,
With might anew, we rise, transcend.

Phoenix Rising

From ashes cold, the fire ignites,
A blaze born from the darkest nights,
Wings unfurled in dawn's first light,
The Phoenix soars to towering heights.

With every fall, the flame renews,
A timeless dance of crimson hues,
Through embered skies, past hidden views,
The spirit lives, defies the blues.

In fiery bursts, it sheds the past,
No chains can bind, no pain can last,
A legend's tale from depths amassed,
Forever free, unsurpassed.

Eternal flames in hearts reside,
In shadows deep, they do not hide,
Like Phoenix, through the storm they'll glide,
To rise again, with grace and pride.

Each end a start, each scream a song,
The journey fierce, the spirit strong,
Through trial's blaze where souls belong,
The Phoenix rose, and thus we throng.

Gentle Rebirth

In whispered winds, the change is near,
A soft embrace to quell our fear,
Through petals blown, we persevere,
In nature's arms, rebirth is clear.

The seasons turn, new life will bloom,
In colors bright, dispelling gloom,
The world reweaves a brighter loom,
In every breath, a vast new room.

From tender shoots to towering trees,
Life springs anew with subtle ease,
A painting brushed by whispered breeze,
With gentle love that never flees.

In quiet night, the stars align,
To guide us through the vast design,
In darkness deep, a light will shine,
And show the way to paths divine.

Through gentle rebirth, hearts ascend,
In shared embrace, wounds start to mend,
In cycles pure, where dreams extend,
We find our place, where spirits blend.

Heart's Revival

In shadows cast, where sorrow dwelled,
A flicker sparked, as darkness quelled,
Through fractured heart, where pain had swelled,
A tender touch, where love had held.

A whispered hope in morning's grace,
Revived the soul in warm embrace,
With every beat, a steady pace,
Renewal found, in sacred space.

Through trials faced and battles long,
A melody, a healing song,
In heart's revival, we belong,
To rise anew, resilient, strong.

The scars, now marks of battles won,
A testament to what's begun,
In every heart, the war is done,
Embrace the light, with each new dawn.

In silent prayer, in deepest sigh,
Our spirits soar, no longer shy,
In heart's revival, dreams can fly,
Together whole, beneath the sky.

Breath of Tranquility

On gentle breeze, the silence sings,
A lullaby on tender wings,
With every breath, the calm it brings,
A world at peace, where spirit clings.

In tranquil woods, where shadows play,
The golden rays of dawning day,
In stillness found, we choose to stay,
And let the chaos drift away.

Through mountain highs and valleys low,
A river's course, in gentle flow,
In nature's arms, our spirits grow,
And find the peace that soothes the soul.

The ocean's waves, a rhythmic beat,
Where sky and water softly meet,
In breath of tranquility, so sweet,
We find a life that's pure, complete.

In silent night, 'neath starry dome,
In tranquil breath, we find our home,
Together, yet we're free to roam,
In harmony, we're not alone.

Aromas of Sanctuary

In gardens where the roses bend,
A scent of peace, where wounds may mend.
A breath, a pause, where spirits blend,
Aroma's grace, on breeze ascend.

Through whispered leaves, the refuge found,
In solace dense, where hearts are crowned.
Embrace the air, the quiet sound,
In sacred spaces, peace is bound.

Beneath the oak, the shadows play,
In twilight's arms, where dreams can stay.
A tender hush from night to day,
In fragrant night, our fears allay.

In sanctuary's sweet perfume,
Where burdens cease and roses bloom,
In scent's embrace, dispel the gloom,
Our weary souls find gentle room.

Tapestries of Self-Love

Threads of gold and silver spun,
Weaving stories, dreams begun.
In mirrors soft, the light of sun,
A tapestry where hearts are won.

Each stitch a tale, a truth unfurled,
Embracing flaws within this world,
Through doubts and fears, love stays uncurled,
Self-love's embrace, a flag unfurled.

Colors blend, no two the same,
A pattern rich in life's hard game.
In every thread, we find our name,
In woven paths, we stake our claim.

Wrap yourself in colors bright,
In warm embrace through darkest night.
The tapestry of pure delight,
Where self-love's glow creates new light.

Shattered Mirrors, Mended Hearts

In shards that gleam from bitter past,
Reflecting hopes that couldn't last.
Yet in those pieces lies a cast,
Of hearts reborn, horizons vast.

Fragments speak of battles fought,
In silver slivers, lessons caught.
Through cracks, new life where hope is sought,
In broken glass, new strength is wrought.

From chaos blooms a mending art,
A tender touch to make us part.
In every break, a healing start,
As shattered mirrors mend the heart.

With care, the pieces re-align,
Creating forms profoundly fine.
In healed mosaic, we find the sign,
Of hearts renewed, in bonds divine.

Eclipses of Pain, Sunrises of Joy

In shadows deep where sorrows lie,
An eclipse darkens, hides the sky.
Our tears like rain, they fall and sigh,
Yet dawn awaits, a hopeful cry.

Through nights of pain, the stars remain,
A distant light through sorrow's reign.
In darkest times, the lessons gain,
From heartache's grasp, we break the chain.

The sky awakes, a burst of light,
Sunrise claims the edge of night.
In golden hues, our spirits fight,
To cast away the shadow's bite.

Joy arrives on morning's breath,
A promise made, defying death.
In every dawn, we feel the depth,
Of pain eclipsed by joy's warm breadth.

Valleys of Solace

In quiet lands where shadows rest,
The sun sets low, a golden crest,
Mountains whisper secrets old,
In valleys deep where peace unfolds.

Gentle streams with gentle song,
Carry dreams where hearts belong,
Fields of green in twilight's grace,
Paint a calm on night's embrace.

Stars appear in velvet skies,
A dance of light before our eyes,
In these valleys, sorrow fades,
Replaced by calm and tranquil shades.

Nature's breath, a soothing touch,
In valleys' hold, it means so much,
Solace found in earth's embrace,
Here, we find our sacred place.

Winds of time, forever weave,
A tapestry of dawn and eve,
In these valleys, we will find,
A solace deep within our mind.

Revolutions of the Heart

Beneath the moon's enchanting glow,
Whispers soft, where rivers flow,
Hearts ignite in midnight's fire,
With every beat, love's desire.

Through ages lost and futures bright,
Love revolves, a timeless light,
Spirals of a heartfelt dance,
Caught within a fleeting glance.

In cycles vast, no start or end,
Love transforms, becomes a friend,
Evolves in silence, blooms in night,
A revolution pure and right.

A spark can fuel a fiery blaze,
Love's revolution never sways,
From hearts once shattered, comes anew,
A love reborn, forever true.

Through every turn, each twist of fate,
Love's power never dissipates,
In revolutions, love takes flight,
A sacred dance in endless night.

Shades of Becoming

In shadows deep, where minds explore,
Lie secrets we forever store,
Through shades and hues of life we tread,
Leaving trails of words unsaid.

From dawn to dusk, our truths we seek,
In every glance, a story peek,
As moments shift, our hearts incline,
To shades that form a grand design.

Becoming through the tides of time,
In prose and rhyme, in steep and climb,
Each challenge faced, each joy embraced,
Shapes who we are in life's haste.

Between the lines of night and day,
We find a path, we find our way,
Through every shade, a truth unveiled,
Through every trial, a spirit hailed.

As morning breaks, as night descends,
Our journey twists, but never ends,
In shades of becoming, we all find,
The endless journey of the mind.

Oceans of Forgiveness

In waves that crash and tides that swell,
Lie secrets in the ocean's spell,
Beneath the blue, where dreams reside,
Forgiveness flows with every tide.

In depths profound, where silence sings,
A soothing balm that healing brings,
For hearts that break and tears that fall,
The ocean's song will mend them all.

Each wave that comes, a whispered plea,
For wounds to heal, for souls to be,
The ocean takes, the pain we give,
Transforms it so that we may live.

Glistening in the morning sun,
Forgiveness shines for everyone,
In every crest and every wave,
Lie chances new, to be brave.

As tides recede, as waters part,
Forgiveness blooms within the heart,
In oceans vast where peace is found,
Our spirits rise, no longer bound.

Expressions of Spirit

In the dance of twilight's kiss,
Whispers of an ancient lore,
Heartfelt dreams, pure and bliss,
Spirit's journey to adore.

In the wind and in the rain,
Voices of the past embrace,
Echoes swell in sweet refrain,
As time reveals a hidden grace.

A song of love, a tune of life,
Gentle waves upon the shore,
An end to sorrow, end to strife,
Where soul and spirit both explore.

In fleeting moments, truth aligns,
The whispering winds do play,
Guiding hearts and open minds,
Towards the break of a new day.

Boundless skies, eternal quest,
Stories carved in stardust bright,
Expressions of the spirit dressed,
In the tapestry of night.

Timeless Echoes

When ages pass in quiet grace,
Echoes of the past remain,
Time's gentle touch on every face,
Whispers of love's grand refrain.

Moments lost yet memories keep,
Silent songs in hearts enshrined,
As we wander through this deep,
Timeless echoes intertwine.

Seas may rise and mountains fall,
Yet within the shadows dance,
Echoes answer every call,
Guiding us through time's expanse.

In the twilight's fading glow,
Stories old, yet ever new,
Timeless echoes gently flow,
Bridging past and future too.

In the stillness of the night,
Every star a timeless guide,
Echoes of eternal light,
Illuminate the path inside.

Stars in a Darkened Sky

Beneath the veil of endless night,
Stars do whisper tales untold,
Each spark a beacon of pure light,
Guiding hearts both brave and bold.

In the tapestry of dreams,
Constellations weave their song,
Silver whispers, moonlit beams,
With the universe we belong.

Darkened skies, a canvass vast,
Infinite in mystery,
Stars like memories of the past,
Guarding silent history.

In their light, we find our way,
Through the shadows we endure,
Stars in darkened skies convey,
Hope and truth forever pure.

Timeless keepers, silent guides,
In their glow, we see afar,
Bound by threads the night provides,
Dreamers follow every star.

Echoes in the Calm

In the quiet of the dawn's embrace,
Echoes drift on morning's breath,
Whispers in this tranquil space,
Life and time in gentle death.

Silent ripples cross the stream,
Echoes of a peaceful past,
In each drop, a scattered dream,
Moments cherished, made to last.

Through the forest, whispers sigh,
Leaves and branches softly speak,
Echoes in the calm comply,
Songs of nature, mild and meek.

In the stillness of the night,
Crickets chirp their timeless tune,
Echoes dance in soft moonlight,
Beneath the watchful, silver moon.

In these echoes, hearts find peace,
Calm within the world's great storm,
From our worries, sweet release,
In the echoes, spirits warm.

Sacred Whispers of Truth

In shadows cast where secrets hide,
A silent whisper speaks the tide.
Of ancient tales and hidden lore,
The essence of truth, forevermore.

Gentle breezes carry thoughts,
Across the plains where dreams are caught.
With every word, the veil doth lift,
Revealing lies in truth's own gift.

The stars above do glimmer bright,
A beacon in the darkest night.
For those who seek, for those who find,
The sacred whispers of the mind.

In sacred groves and temples old,
The stories of the brave and bold.
Each echoing word, each hallowed breath,
Brings forth a light, dispelling death.

Horizons Unbound

Beyond the hills where sun meets land,
A new horizon, vast and grand.
With every dawn, a chance anew,
To chase the dreams that are but few.

The sky, a canvas painted wide,
With colors bold and stars as guide.
Each step we take, each path we tread,
Moves us forward, firmly led.

Through fields of green and oceans blue,
The world unravels from our view.
Unbound by time, unchained by past,
The future calls, the die is cast.

Mountains high and valleys low,
The journey's path, forever flows.
In every heart, in every soul,
Horizons unbound, make us whole.

Halls of Inner Peace

Within the heart, a tranquil space,
A place of calm, a sacred place.
Where thoughts converge in gentle streams,
And silence holds our deepest dreams.

Each heartbeat echoes harmony,
A rhythm of serenity.
In every breath, in every sigh,
The halls of peace, we sanctify.

Among the whispers, soft and kind,
A refuge for the weary mind.
In moments still, the spirit finds,
A solace in these peaceful binds.

In shadows light, in darkness bright,
All burdens lift and take their flight.
The sacred halls, within they gleam,
In inner peace, we find our dream.

Tides of Serenity

By oceans deep, where waters flow,
A gentle tide, in tranquil glow.
It speaks of calm, it sings of peace,
A symphony that will not cease.

The waves arise, the waves do fall,
A timeless dance that soothes us all.
With every crest, with every break,
The soul finds rest, for calm's own sake.

The moon above, with silver light,
Illuminates the tranquil night.
Its glow upon the waters clear,
Instills in us a sense of cheer.

In every tide, in every wave,
A piece of calm, we surely crave.
For in the ebb and flow we see,
The gentle tides of serenity.

Quests for Tranquility

In whispering woods, where shadows play,
The weary heart finds its way,
Beneath the boughs of ancient trees,
A refuge made with nature's ease.

By gentle streams that softly flow,
The murmurs cleanse the soul below,
In quietude, the spirits mend,
Embarking on that tranquil bend.

Through misty fields where lilies bloom,
Escaping from encroaching gloom,
The journey long, yet wisdom's key,
Unlocks the path to serenity.

On mountain trails so high and vast,
With winds that whisper of the past,
The quest for peace through valleys green,
A goal within the soul unseen.

In every dawn, new hope reborn,
In every dusk, the calm adorn,
Through life's deep quests for tranquil light,
The heart finds peace both day and night.

Fractured Light

In shards of dawn the morning breaks,
The silence of the night forsakes,
With colors spilling pure and bright,
Emerging from the fractured light.

Through prisms seen with eyes anew,
The world revealed in every hue,
A tapestry of dreams untold,
In fragile beams of sunlight gold.

As twilight whispers softly spread,
The sunbeams whisper, softly shed,
Translucent hues of fleeting might,
They wane within the fractured light.

In moonlit eves where shadows bound,
The fractured light on water found,
Reflecting dreams in silvery streams,
The night unfolds with secret dreams.

Yet in the heart, a lingering glow,
From scattered beams that ebb and flow,
Through fractured light, the soul finds sight,
In broken brilliance, pure delight.

Whole Soul

Amid the chaos strongly spun,
Where threads of life and time have run,
A heart alone, a spirit free,
Seeking out its destiny.

Through valleys deep and mountains high,
Beneath the ever-watchful sky,
A journey taken step by step,
To knit the soul where shadows wept.

In quiet reflection, soft repose,
Where inner strength and courage grows,
A wholeness born from fractured parts,
A unity of aching hearts.

The cracks and scars of years before,
Now form a mosaic to adore,
With every loss, a beauty shown,
A testament to how we've grown.

Whole soul, complete, in light it strays,
Through winding paths and endless days,
In every beat, a life well-spun,
A tapestry of what we've won.

Paintbrushes of Memory

With paintbrushes of memory,
We canvas dreams of reverie,
In strokes of joy and shades of sorrow,
Painting pasts that shape our morrow.

Each hue a story, each line a lore,
Of days behind, of hearts that soar,
The portraits drawn from time's embrace,
In every color, find our place.

Scenes of laughter, tinted bright,
Moments washed in soft moonlight,
In sepia tones of distant days,
The brushstrokes dance in gleaming rays.

Amidst the galleries of our minds,
A legacy of frames entwined,
In every masterpiece we see,
The whispered traces of what could be.

Thus in the art of lived-out dreams,
The canvas of our life redeems,
Paintbrushes of memory,
Sketching out eternity.

Bridges to Wholeness

Across the chasms, deep and wide,
In life's long quest for hearts to guide,
We build with hope the arching spans,
That link our souls through time's demands.

The stones of strength, the beams of trust,
In daylight's warmth, in nights of dust,
Each bridge a pathway to the core,
Where broken pieces heal once more.

In every arch, a story told,
In every step, a journey bold,
We walk the paths of pain and joy,
Connecting dreams we once employed.

Through storms that shake the very ground,
These bridges hold, their strength unbound,
A testament to love's embrace,
That time and trials cannot erase.

So let us build with hearts sincere,
These bridges spanning far and near,
For in their crossing, we find peace,
A wholeness born from sweet release.

Ember to Flame

From ember's glow in shadowed night,
There springs a warmth, subdued, yet bright.
A spark that whispers, yearning, seeks
To blaze and roar with fierce peaks.

A gust of wind, a breath of air,
Turns whispers into future's flare.
As embers wake, in fiery claim,
Transmute the night from ember to flame.

In patience waits the strongest heat,
For moments grand, its pulse to beat.
The phoenix from the ashes rise,
Their fervor lighting darkened skies.

Petals of Peace

In gardens where tranquility blooms,
Peace drifts on petals, scents in plumes.
A dance of color, soft and clear,
Whispers calm, and all, endear.

Among the leaves, a hush prevails,
Each breath of harmony unveils.
A gentle world where silence sings,
On nature's breeze, serenity springs.

In morning's light or twilight's fall,
Peace unfurls, embracing all.
Where petals touch, the heart finds ease,
Resting in this gentle, verdant peace.

Journey Toward Light

In shadows' grip we start our quest,
Through trials which our hearts invest.
Each step toward dawn, with aim so slight,
Guides us forth, from night to light.

The path, though darkened, we shall trod,
With faith our compass, hope our rod.
The stars, they whisper, flickering bright,
Beacons on our journey toward light.

Through valleys deep and mountains tall,
We climb, we strive, refusing fall.
For in our hearts, a flame ignites,
Leading forth, to broader sights.

Silent Triumphs

In stillness lies a quiet strength,
A force unseen at heart's great length.
Not in the shout or battle cry,
But whispered winds that strengthen, fly.

The sun's ascent, a tranquil rise,
In calm, emboldens distant skies.
With grace, the world in silence sighs,
Its victories not in loud goodbyes.

Unheralded, these wins unfold,
In quiet acts, both brave and bold.
For silent triumphs, subtle, true,
Reveal the strength in me, in you.

Echoes of Self-Kindness

In the mirror's soft reflection,
A gentle soul does start to see.
Each scar, a tale of resurrection,
Whispering, 'You are truly free.'

In moments fraught with doubt and fear,
A heart finds solace in its song.
Embrace the voice, hold it dear,
For with self-love, we grow strong.

When shadows creep in silent night,
And burdens seem too much to bear,
Remember, you are your own light—
A lantern in the world's despair.

Cherish every fragile part,
The pieces that you often miss.
In the boundless depths of heart,
Find strength in your soul's tender kiss.

A journey vast and undefined,
With every step comes healing's grace.
In echoes of self-kindness, find
The courage to embrace your place.

Lanterns in the Dark

In the night when stars are hidden,
And dreams are veiled in deep mystery,
A lantern's glow, a hope unbidden,
Guides the spirit toward tranquility.

Silent whispers through the gloom,
Softly call from shadowed trees.
Amidst the darkness, flowers bloom,
Their scent a balm on every breeze.

Eyes will open to the dim,
Each glint a beacon, subtle shine.
In the space where fears do swim,
A lantern shapes a hopeful line.

Footsteps trace the winding trail,
In company of unseen grace.
As night-time stories weave and pale,
A lantern lights each hidden place.

So carry forth through dusk's embrace,
Let courage rise from spark and flame.
In lanterns' glow, find your own space,
A light that bears your cherished name.

Unveiled Horizons

Through the mist of early dawning,
Soft horizons start to wake.
In the calm of day's first yawning,
New paths and dreams we gently take.

Mountains rise in hues of gold,
Unveiled by sun's unerring grace.
Each step ahead, a future bold,
As we embrace the open space.

In valleys deep and rivers wide,
Life's wonders call with voices clear.
The world unfolds where dreams reside,
Each moment free from doubt and fear.

Onward through untrodden fields,
With every dawn, a promise new.
The journey's gifts and all it yields,
Bind hearts to skies of endless blue.

Horizons stretch to meet our gaze,
In endless dance of light and time.
Unveiled, the threads of hope and praise,
A testament in every rhyme.

Timeless Embrace

In the folds of time, love lingers,
With whispered vows and soft caress.
A bond that slips through fleeting fingers,
Yet holds a heart in soul's recess.

Ancient stories blend with now,
Through ages worn, their truth remains.
In timeless embrace, we learn the vow,
Of love that flows through endless veins.

Moments fleet yet deeply root,
Memories stitched in tender seams.
In heart's embrace, all fears are moot,
Love remains in life's grand themes.

Through the storms and through the calm,
Hands find hands in silent plea.
In timeless embrace, there's a balm,
That heals with love's eternity.

A rhythm pure and ever steady,
Through the years and through the change.
In hearts held close and always ready,
Love's a timeless, boundless range.

Sea of Wholeness

In depths where silence sings,
The ocean's heart does beat.
Ripples in moonlit rings,
A dance so calm, so fleet.

Waves whisper ancient tales,
Of life both near and far.
Where twilight gently pales,
Guided by northern star.

The sea, a cloak of blue,
Holds secrets in its fold.
A world both old and new,
With treasures yet untold.

Beneath its tranquil face,
A symphony awakes.
With every gentle trace,
The soul of water quakes.

Eternal vast expanse,
In wholeness, we admire.
To watch the waves and dance,
In dreams we dare aspire.

Graceful Returns

When daylight starts to fade,
And dusk begins to weep.
Shadows in twilight's shade,
Gently lay me to sleep.

The moon with silver gleams,
In night's soft, velvet shawl.
Whispers return in dreams,
A silent, graceful call.

Stars blink like eyes above,
Watching o'er our quest.
Embraced by night's true love,
In stillness, we find rest.

We journey back in time,
Through memories alight.
Each step a heartfelt rhyme,
In the tender quiet night.

Come morning's gentle sway,
We rise, as dawn confirms.
In light of a new day,
To face life's graceful returns.

Sanctuary Within

In the quiet of the mind,
A haven lies concealed.
Peace we often strive to find,
By grace, it is revealed.

Amid the storm's embrace,
A calm ignites within.
A sanctuary's face,
Where true serenity begins.

Mountains high and valleys low,
Through life's vast terrain.
The heart will come to know,
Its refuge from all pain.

Beauty in the still,
Whispers soft and clear.
The soul can drink its fill,
Of love that conquers fear.

No need to search afar,
For peace that dreams have sought.
In the heart, our guiding star,
Sanctuary is wrought.

Milton Keynes UK
Ingram Content Group UK Ltd.
UKHW021950210624
444498UK00015B/364